LIGHTNING BOLT BOOKS™

Unusual Traits:
Tongue Rolling, Special Taste Sensors, and More

Buffy Silverman

Lerner Publications Company
Minneapolis

To Jake:
Eyebrow raiser,
ear wiggler, and
tongue roller
extraordinaire!
—B. S.

Lerner Publications Company
A division of Lerner Publishing Group, Inc.
241 First Avenue North
Minneapolis, MN 55401 U.S.A.

Website address: www.lernerbooks.com

Library of Congress Cataloging-in-Publication Data

Silverman, Buffy.
      Unusual traits : tongue rolling, special taste sensors, and more / by Buffy Silverman.
          p.   cm. — (Lightning bolt books™ — What traits are in your genes?)
      Includes index.
      ISBN 978–0–7613–8943–9 (lib. bdg. : alk. paper)
      1. Human genetics — Variation — Juvenile literature. I. Title.
      QH431.S624 2013
      599.93'5 — dc23   2011045553

Manufactured in the United States of America
1 — CG — 7/15/12

Table of Contents

Traits **page 4**

Can You Taste This? **page 10**

Can You Do This? **page 17**

Can You Smell This? **page 22**

Activity **page 28**

Glossary **page 30**   Further Reading **page 31**   Index **page 32**

Traits

Look at these children.
Each child looks different.

Our differences are called traits. People have many different traits.

Eye color is a trait. Height is a trait too.

Your body has directions for traits. These directions are called genes.

You follow directions to build a model. Genes are directions for your body.

Genes tell your body how to work and grow. You got your genes from your birth parents.

Birth parents are related to a child. Adoptive parents bring a child into their family and become the child's parents.

Genes come in pairs. One of each pair came from your mom. The other came from your dad. Your genes make you different from other people.

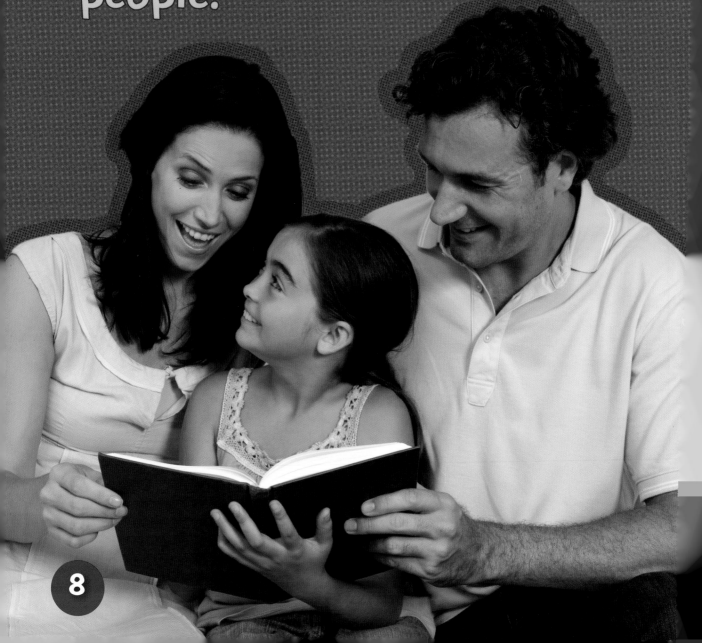

Every person is different. But we also share many traits. We run on two legs. We use our hands to draw.

People have more in common with one another than they do with dogs and other animals.

Can You Taste This?

Do you have freckles? Traits such as freckles are easy to see.

Other traits are hidden. You might like different foods than your friend. You can't tell that by looking at each other.

Do you like broccoli?

If not, your genes may be the reason. A chemical called **PTC** is in broccoli. Your genes control whether you can taste **PTC**.

The gene for tasting PTC comes in two forms. The different forms of a gene are called alleles. One allele makes PTC taste bitter. The other allele doesn't react to PTC.

If you have two copies of the allele that doesn't react to PTC, you do not taste it.

These kids are licking paper with **PTC**. One thinks *yuck!* He has an allele that lets him taste **PTC**. The other kid cannot taste it.

People test their genes for PTC by tasting special paper. This boy doesn't like the taste.

This boy got an allele from his mom for tasting PTC. His dad passed along an allele that doesn't react to PTC. The PTC-tasting allele takes control. The boy can taste PTC.

This boy thinks broccoli tastes bitter.

You might not like broccoli. But someday you may like it. Some people learn to like new tastes.

Can You Do This?

Try to roll your tongue into a U-shape. Can you do it? Or does your tongue stay flat?

17

Genes play a part in tongue rolling. Many people roll their tongues easily. Others can roll their tongues a little. Some people cannot roll their tongues.

Sometimes people can learn to roll their tongues with practice. Scientists aren't sure how genes control this trait.

Can you read the word on the truck below? This is called mirror writing. The word appears normal in a mirror. Very few people can write like this.

In mirror writing, the letters are backward. But drivers can clearly read the word on this truck when they see it in their rearview mirrors.

Are you good at mirror writing? If so, one of your parents is probably good at it too. Genes play a part in this trait.

Can You Smell This?

Imagine the smell of brownies. People like some foods because of their smell.

But not everyone smells the same smells. Your genes let you smell certain scents.

23

Most people smell a funny odor after they eat asparagus. And the smell is in a funny place. It's in their pee! But some people smell nothing.

Scientists found that there are two different traits. The first trait is whether you make the odor. The second trait is whether you can smell it.

Hundreds of genes control our sense of smell. People have different alleles of these genes. So everyone smells things differently.

Your genes are part of what makes you special.

What special traits
do you have?

Activity

Track the Traits!

Track the different traits in your classroom. List these traits on a sheet of lined paper:

can taste **PTC** paper
can't taste **PTC** paper

can roll tongue
can't roll tongue

can mirror write
can't mirror write

Then divide your paper into two columns. One column will be for the traits. The other column will be for tally marks. (You'll find out what tally marks are and how to use them next.) Your paper should look like the sample sheet on page 29 when you're done.

Put a tally mark next to each trait that you have. A tally mark is a straight up-and-down line, like this:

|

Then ask your classmates about their traits. Make a tally mark for each classmate next to his or her traits. When you get to five, put a diagonal line through your tally marks, like this:

That's how you write the number five in tally marks. For the number six, make a new tally mark, like this:

When you're done tallying the traits, count how many of you have each trait. Which traits got the most tallies?

Sample Sheet:

Traits	Tally Marks
can taste PTC paper	
can't taste PTC paper	
can roll tongue	
can't roll tongue	
can mirror write	
can't mirror write	

Note: If you don't have PTC paper available, you can still have fun tracking traits! Just ask your classmates about tongue rolling and mirror writing. You can always try the PTC test another time.

Glossary

allele: one of two or more forms of a gene

asparagus: a green, spear-shaped vegetable that is cooked and eaten

birth parent: a parent that is genetically related to a child

broccoli: a plant with green flower buds and stalks. Broccoli can be eaten cooked or raw.

freckle: a small, light brown spot on your skin

gene: one of the parts of the cells of all living things. Genes are passed from parents to children and determine how you look and the way you grow.

mirror writing: writing from right to left with backward letters. Mirror writing looks normal in a mirror.

PTC: a chemical that some people taste as bitter and others do not. PTC stands for phenylthiocarbamide.

trait: a quality or characteristic that makes one person or thing different from another

Further Reading

Harris, Trudy. *Tally Cat Keeps Track.* Minneapolis: Millbrook Press, 2011.

Muse Experiments: Asparagus Pee
http://www.musemagkids.com
/experiments/asparagus-pee

PBS Kids Go!: Tongue Rollers
http://pbskids.org/zoom
/activities/sci/tonguerollers.html

Silverman, Buffy. *Hair Traits: Color, Texture, and More.* Minneapolis: Lerner Publications Company, 2013.

Simpson, Kathleen. *Genetics: From DNA to Designer Dogs.* Washington, DC: National Geographic, 2008.

What Makes You You?
http://www.amnh.org/ology/features/stufftodo
_genetics/youquiz.php?TB_iframe=true&height
=540&width=600

Index

alleles, 13–15, 26

birth parents, 7

genes, 6–8, 12–13, 18–19, 21, 23, 26–27

mirror writing, 20–21

PTC, 12–15

scientists, 19, 25
smell, 22–26

taste, 12–16
tongue rolling, 17–19
traits, 5–6, 9–11, 19, 21, 25, 27

Photo Acknowledgments

The images in this book are used with the permission of: © Hemera/Thinkstock, p. 1 (both); © Hughstoneian/Dreamstime.com, p. 2; © Flirt/SuperStock, p. 4; © Jacek Chabraszewski/Dreamstime.com, p. 5; © Purestock/Getty Images, p. 6; © SelectStock/ the Agency Collection/Getty Images, p. 7; © B2M/Photographer's Choice RF/Getty Images, p. 8; © Peter Zander/Workbook Stock/Getty Images, p. 9; © Todd Strand/ Independent Picture Service, pp. 10, 14 (both), 21; © Digital Vision/Getty Images, p. 11; © Jupiterimages/Comstock Images/Getty Images, p. 12; © Jose Luis Pelaez Inc/Blend Images/Getty Images, p. 13; © iStockphoto.com/Andrew Rich, p. 15; © JGI/Jamie Grill/ Getty Images, p. 16; © Janine Wiedel Photolibrary/Alamy, p. 17; © Graham Dunn/ Alamy, p. 18; © Jan Greune/LOOK/Getty Images, p. 19; © Zimmytws/Dreamstime.com, p. 20; © iStockphoto.com/TheCrimsonMonkey, p. 22; © Monkeybusinessimages/ Dreamstime.com, p. 23; © Steve Skjold/age fotostock/SuperStock, p. 24; © Steph Fowler/Brand X Pictures/Getty Images, p. 25; © David R. Frazier Photolibrary, Inc/ Alamy, p. 26; © Brand X Pictures/Jupiterimages/Thinkstock, p. 27; © KidStock/Blend Images/Getty Images, p. 31.

Front cover: © Palmer Kane LLC/Shutterstock.com (top); © Todd Strand/Independent Picture Service (bottom).

Main body text set in Johann Light 30/36.